# Weight Watc

## *Freesty*

## Cookbook 2018 WITHDRAWN

Discover how to lose weight fast with this Ultimate, All New
Weight watchers Freestyle Recipes!

Daniel Fisher

River Forest Public Library
735 Lathrop Avenue
River Forest, IL 60305
708-366-5205    em
**January**  2019  3c

Copyright page

ISBN-13: 978-1-948191-33-3

ISBN-10: 1-948191-33-4

Copyright © 2018 by Original Life-Saver Publishers

All rights reserved. This book or any portion thereof may not be reproduced or used in any manner whatsoever without the express written permission of the publisher except for the use of brief quotations in a book review.

Printed in The U.S.A

# Table of Contents

I want to personally Congratulate you and thank you for Purchasing my book " Weight Watchers Freestyle Cookbook 2018: *Discover how to lose weight fast with this Ultimate, All New Weight watchers Freestyle Recipes!*"

This is the only book you'll need to lose those stubborn fats this year. You'll Discover the New Weight watchers plan everyone is talking about, Freestyle and Flex. Also, there are New, tasty and healthy Recipes that are easy to make and will help you achieve your weight loss goal. We also included a Smart Weekly Planner to help you plan your meals every week. The Freestyle and Flex Plan will Jumpstart your New Weight loss goal and we believe in no time, you'll lose those Fat rapidly. Now let's get Started!

# Introduction

Weight watchers is a diet plan aimed at those who are looking to lose weight, without eliminating certain food groups. Weight watchers have a point value for every food, and those points are known as Weight watchers Smartpoints.

## Weight watchers Freestyle Plan

According to the Weight Watcher Site, these new addition provide a foundation in which members can build a healthy pattern of eating. The foods were selected because they provide high quality nutrition and also form the basis of a healthy diet without posing a risk of over indulgence, thereby making it easier for one to pay attention to when satisfied as opposed to overeating.

Weight watchers freestyle plan is based on SmartPoints System, which encourages the consumption of fruits, vegetables, lean proteins and less sugars. This new program was launched in the last month of 2017.

It is an expansion of Smartpoint and 'Behind the scale' which was released three years ago. Under the old plan, every food had a smart point value- with majority of the vegetables having smart point values. The new plan is an expansion of the food points list to include lean proteins. The Smartpoints budget is customized for each member based on their age, weight, height, and gender. All information would be gotten during sign up into weight watchers, and then personal daily points tailored for each person.

Even though it seems like a mix between Smartpoint and simply filling (weight watchers no point option), there are some noticeable differences between both plans. In Freestyle:

- Daily smart points budgets are given, so also are weekly smart point for excess.

- There is a zero point food list, which includes eggs, corn, boneless chicken breast, vegetables, lentils, tofu, and sea food. Roll over points- Up to four Smartpoints roll over, into weeklies, on the condition that one tracks an item a day which has to be less than four.

- Less tracking, the added food values doesn't need to be weighed or tracked. Hence the flexibility of the new weight program.

- Due to the expanded zero smart points food list, daily smart points are adjusted- reduced, to balance out the zero points food addition and account for the extra calories that may accumulate as a result of the unlimited foods.

- There are over two hundred newly added zero smart points items.

- It has a 14 point range.

Whereas in Simply filling:

- The Smartpoints budget is weekly Smartpoints only.

- Simply filling allows a broader list free foods (foods one is allowed to select on their own); the freestyle zero smartpoints foods, whole grains, cheese, reduced-calorie bread, red meat, healthy oil etc.

- Simply filling doesn't permit roll overs.

The goal of the weight watchers freestyle plan is to give people the free rein to eat whatever they enjoy, bearing in mind that one is less likely to stray from the diet that they enjoy. It has also been shown that people have a certain reserve toward weight loss plans that restrict certain food classes.

The Freestyle plan uses the Smartpoint. The Smartpoints is a counting system adopted from the Propoints system. It encourages members to make healthier, nutritious choices by eating less sugar and saturated fat and simply counting calories. With foods higher in sugar or saturated fats having higher Smartpoints values, and foods higher in lean proteins, lower Smartpoints values, members are nudged toward healthier eating choices.

- Here, every food is assigned its own Smartpoint values based on its composition of calories, protein, saturated fat and sugar.

- Foods rich in protein have lower Smartpoints value.

- Saturated fat and Sugar increases Smartpoints value.

- Smartpoints are easy to track as they are calculated in whole numbers, and can be tracked with some tools.

The Freestyle Smartpoint system uses the latest nutritional and weight loss science to make healthy eating as flexible (one is not constricted by dieting) and easy as possible. Every food and drink have a Smartpoints value, a number that is based on calories, protein, sugar and saturated fat.

Each day, a Smartpoint budget is given, to be used on any food item as desired. Your age, height, weight, and gender, is calculated based on the Daily smartpoints budget, with 23 being the minimum daily value. Only the foods with smart point values need to be track. One, is only expected to track the foods with Smartpoints value. All zero smartpoints foods aren't required to be tracked.

Each week, a weekly smartpoint budget (weeklies) is given-this is given in the instance one's daily smartpoints budgets have been exceeded. This way you can be able to lose weight easily.

# How to Add The Zero Point Food to Your Diet

The New Weight watchers plan is making losing weight very easy, they have included lots of yummy foods you'll enjoy; this include plant based protein sources like turkey, eggs, tofu, chicken, lentils, yogurt and beans with lean animal inclusive. In addition, you'll get to enjoy your favorite sweetcorn and peas freely on the new plans.

200 New Zero Point Food List:

Apple

Applesauce

Apricots

Arrowroot

Artichoke hearts

Artichokes

Arugula

Asparagus

Bamboo shoots

Banana

Beans

Beets

Berries

Blackberries

Blueberries

Broccoli

Broccoli rabe

Broccoli slaw'

Broccolini

Brussels sprouts

Cabbage

Calamari

Cantaloupe

Carrots

Cauliflower

Caviar

Celery

Swiss chard

Chicken breast(fat free)

Chicken breast or tenderloin

Clementines

Coleslaw mix

Collards

Corn

Cranberries

Cucumber

Daikon

Dates

Dragon fruit

Edamame

Egg substitutes

Egg whites

Eggplant

Eggs (whole)

Endive

Escarole

Fennel

Figs

Fish

Fish fillet

Fruit cocktail

Fruit cup

Fruit salad

Fruit

Garlic

Ginger root

Grape fruit

Grapes

Greens

Greens, mixed baby

Guavas

Guava, Strawberry

Hearts of palm

Honey dew melon

Jack fruit

Jerk Chicken Breast

Jerusalem artichokes

Jicama

Kiwifruit

Kohlrabi

Kumquats

Leeks

Lemon

Lemon zest

Lentils

Lettuce

Lime

Lime zest

Litchis

Mangoes

Melon balls

Mung bean sprouts

Mung dal

Mushroom caps

Mushrooms

Nectarine

Nori seaweed

Okra

Onions

Oranges

Papayas

Parseley

Passion fruit

Pea shoots

Peaches

Peapods, black-eye

Pears

Peas and carrots

Peas

Peppers

Pepperoncini

Persimmons

Pickles

Pico de gallo

Pimientos

Pine apple

Plumcots

Plums

Pomegranates

Pomelo

Pumpkin

Pumpkin puree

Radicchio

Radishes

Raspberries

Rutabagas

Salad, mixed greens

Salad, side (no dressing)

Salad, three-bean

Sala, tossed(no dressing)

Salsa verde

Salsa, fat free

Salsa, fat free, glutton free

Sashimi

Satay, chicken

Satsuma  mandarin

Sauerkraut

Scallions

Seaweed

Shallots

Shellfish

Spinach

Sprouts

Squash, summer

Squash winter

Starfruit

Strawberries

Succotash

Tangelo

Tangerine

Taro

Tofu

Tofu, smoked

Tomatillos

Tomato puree

Tomato sauce

Tomatoes

Turkey breast (ground)

Turkey breast or tenderloin

Turkey breast(skinless)

Turnips

Vegetable sticks

Vegetables, mixed

Vegetables, stir fry

Water chestnuts

Watercress

Watermelon

Yoghurt (Greek)

Yoghurt (plain)

Yoghurt, soy

## How to Use the Activity Points

Activity Points are also known as FitPoints, and can be earned through exercising. This points can be swapped for smart points, thereby increasing the food points one is allowed to eat in a day.

Fitpoints, just like smartpoints are assigned to members upon registration, and the point assigned to the member is based on their weight, age, gender, and activity level. Each member is given a Fitpoints goal for the week, and that increases based on his/her performance in meeting up to those weekly goals. This, the weight watchers do to encourage activity so weight loss is not through dieting alone.

The activity could range from, walking, jogging, running or dancing- as every movement count. The higher the intensity of the activity being performed, the higher the heart rate. The activities intensity (Exercise Intensity Levels) are divided into three as measured by the heart rate.

- High Intensity – Breathing here is labored, and one can only speak in short phrases.

- Moderate intensity- with a heart rate of 93 to 118 beats per minute, breathing is noticeably deeper. One can carry out conversations, but only intermittently.

- Low intensity- There is no noticeable change in the breathing patter, and this activities does not induce sweating.

Any activity done at the following levels are necessary for weight loss. Although the higher the intensity of the activity and the longer time spent doing the exercise, the greater energy expended which implies the greater weight lost.

Activity Points values are calculated using the level of intensity, body weight and time spent exercising to calculate the amount of energy expended.

Weight Watcher Points Calculator is set to calculate the

values based on age, gender, height, weight, and activity

level of the member. Specific points are added based on

those aspects.

Gender

Male= +8

Female =+2

Age

17 – 26years = + 4 points

27- 37years = + 2 points

38 – 47years = +2 points

48- 58years = +1

Weight

Per ten pounds of body weight = +1

Height

5.1ft – 5.10ft = +1 point

> 5.10ft = +2 points

Activity level

High activity= +6 points

Moderate activity = +2 points

Low activity = +0 points

Addition of the above factors gives one the amount of Smartpoints that they are allowed to eat in a day. The points should be recalculated every two to four weeks to account for the weight loss.

To study the amount of points in each food, study the nutritional information of the processed product and divide the total calories and grams of fat by 50 and twelve respectively. Add the numbers together - the nutritional break down of none packaged foods and vegetables can be obtained from online websites or by contacting a nutritionist. Next, divide the total amount of dietary fiber by 5 and subtract from the number gotten by adding the result of the calorie and gram division. Deduct each meal from the total amount of daily points.

An easier method of calculating the points, is by using weight watchers brand meals or recipes.

There are two approaches to losing weight on weight watchers

1. Count Smartpoint approach – this allows one to eat whichever food, using the daily and weekly budgets- giving one the freedom and flexibility of eating whatever they want.

2. No Count Approach/ Freestyle- this allows one a selected list of healthy foods, which should be strictly followed. However, one isn't expected to count or track them – and a weekly allowance for foods not included on the list is given.

In theory, it is believed that about 3500 calories is equivalent to one pound of body weight, and using this as a basis- to lose a pound each week, one must reduce their intake by about 500 calories a day, and by making those changes in one's diet, one can lose an a average of two pounds in a week.

Although this value is not uniform in the subsequent weeks on weight watchers- some weeks one might lose more or less than two pounds, one, however can be certain they're on the right tract if one averages the loss of two pounds at the end of the month (4*2/ 2). The weight lost during the first month is usually rapid due to the body's adjustment to the healthier consumption of food. The weight however been lost is known as the water weight, the body fat requires a longer time to be burned off and hence the need for earning fitpoints.

We have included in this section some wonderful Zero Point Food Ideas You can Start making now that will help you attain maximum weight loss. They are easy to Make you should Try Them.

## Zero Point Breakfast Ideas

- Pumpkin pancakes made with half cup canned pumpkin, Two whisked eggs, and a dash of cinnamon.

- Using a dash of cinnamon, make Banana pancakes with one mashed banana, 2 whisked eggs.

- Two eggs scrambled with half cup black beans and salsa with a side of fruit.

- Roasted veggies that are left over with two poached eggs and half cup lentils.

- One cup nonfat Greek yogurt with fresh fruit and cinnamon

- Cooked ground turkey, Lettuce tacos with taco seasoning and half cup pinto beans, salsa and veggies

- Green salad with turkey breast or cooked chicken

- Nonfat Greek yogurt mixed with Canned tuna, mustard, and hollowed out tomato or diced celery in lettuce wraps

- Leftover cooked fish with lentils and veggies

- Using nonfat Greek yogurt to make Egg salad, mustard, and salad or diced celery in lettuce wraps.

P.S More Recipes in the Printed Book

## Zero Point Dinner Ideas

- Crust less quiche made with veggies, eggs and served with green salad

- Stir-fry with lean chicken or turkey (or tofu), lots of veggies, and soy sauce served with cauliflower rice

- Ground chicken or turkey burgers served in lettuce wraps with bake carrot fries

- Baked salmon with vegetables and chickpeas

- Roasted chicken with lentils and roasted vegetables.

## Zero Point Snack and Dessert Ideas

- Microwave egg mugs

- fruit with Nonfat Greek yogurt

- Banana n'ice cream

- Banana pancakes made with one mashed banana, Two whisked eggs, and a dash of cinnamon for dessert.

# Delicious & Healthy WW Freestyle Recipes

We have made for you lot's of delicious and healthy WW Freestyle Recipes you can start using now.

Most of the recipes contains more of the zero points food, We have limited those foods the will be harmful to your health e.g. Sugar, Grains, labelled Diet Food, Processed Food, Alcohol and deep fried food.

We incorporated most of the healthy foods e.g. Egg, meat, seafoods, fruits, vegetables, nuts and seeds.

We hope you enjoy this meal as much as we do.

Ingredients
4-6 ounces semisweet chocolate morsels

20 pecan halves, toasted

How you make it:

- In a microwave-safe bowl, microwave the chocolate morsels on high until melted, (or for about 1-1 half minutes) or stirring every 30 seconds.

- Then place on a wax paper-lined baking sheet after Dip half of each pecan half in melted chocolate, let cool completely.

- Store in an airtight container for up to 2 days.

Servings: 20 pecans

Nutritional information for one serving:

Freestyle SmartPoints: 1
Calories: 41
Calories from fat: 24
Total fat: 2.8g
Cholesterol: 0mg
Total carbs: 4g

Fiber: 0.6g
Protein: 0.4g

Ingredients
1/2 peach (use canned peach halves in light syrup)
1/3-1/2 cup vanilla yogurt

How you make it

1. Spread the vanilla yogurt into a circle on a plate, using the back of a spoon.
2. In the middle of the yogurt, place down the peach half, flat side.
3. If Additional serving if desired, repeat these steps for each of them.

Makes 1 serving

Nutritional information for one serving:
Freestyle SmartPoints: 0
Calories: 68
Calories from fat: 24
Total fat: 2.8g
Cholesterol: 10mg Fiber: 0.7g
Protein: 3.3g Total carbs: 8.5g

Makes 8 servings
Ingredients


1 (15 ounce) Drained can chickpeas

1/4 cup fresh parsley leaves
1/4 cup orange juice
Two tbsp. tahini (sesame seed paste)
One garlic clove
Two tbsp. chopped onions
Two tbsp. rice vinegar
One tsp Dijon mustard

1/4 tsp ground cumin
One tsp low sodium soy sauce

1/4 tsp ground turmeric
1/4 tsp ground coriander
1/4 tsp paprika

1/4 tsp salt
1/4 tsp ground ginger


How you Make it:


1. In a blender or food processor, Place the garlic, orange juice, onion and parsley and process until

smooth.

2. Add all the remaining ingredients and process until smooth.

3. Serve with raw vegetables or pita triangles.

Freestyle SMARTPOINTS per serving: 1

Nutritional information per serving: 92 calories, 2.5g fat, 2.9g fiber

Makes 4 servings

Ingredients
1 lb sweet potatoes, peeled
1 tablespoon extra-virgin olive oil
1 teaspoon cajun seasoning (or to taste)
salt (to taste)

How you make it:

1. Preheat the oven to 375 degrees F.
2. Quarter the potatoes and cut into 1/4 inch thick strips.
3. Spread the potatoes on a lightly oiled baking sheet, sprinkle with olive oil and Cajun seasoning and toss to coat.
4. Bake in the lower third of the oven for about 30 minutes, stirring occasionally.
5. Season with salt to taste and serve hot.
Freestyle Smartpoint per serving: 2
Nutritional information per serving: 127 calories, 3.4g fat, 3.4g fiber

Makes 4 servings

Ingredients
3/4 lb ground turkey
Two Chopped scallions or green onions

1/3 cup Monterey Jack cheese
One tbsp. ketchup

1/4 tsp garlic powder
One tbsp. soy sauce
1/4 tsp pepper

How you make it:

1. In a bowl, combine all the ingredients (except the cheese).
2. Blend in the cheese.
3. Form into 4 patties.
4. Spray a frying pan with cooking spray.
5. Cook the patties until done.
6. Serve on hamburger buns with lettuce and tomatoes.

Freestyle Smartpoint per serving: 4
Nutritional information per serving: 171 calories, 9.9g fat, 0.3g fiber

Freestyle Squashed Tomatoes
Makes 4 servings


Ingredients
Two cups Big cherry tomatoes
One garlic clove
1/2-1 dried red chili, crumbled (or red pepper flakes)
One tsp extra-virgin olive oil
Four slices country bread
sea salt
freshly ground black pepper


How you make it:


1. Heat the broiler or grill. Set the cooking rack 3 inches from the heat.
2. Place the tomatoes on a rimmed baking pan. Broil them for about 2 minutes (until they soften and the skins start to blister and split).
3. Using tongs, flip the tomatoes and broil them for about 2 more minutes (until blistered but not totally soft).
4. Transfer the tomatoes to a serving dish and lightly squash with a fork so some of the juices run out.
5. Sprinkle with olive oil, chili, salt and pepper; and gently fold to combine.

6. Serve over toasted country bread that has been rubbed with a garlic clove.

WW Freestyle Smartpoints per serving: 1
Nutritional information per serving: 171 calories, 5.3g fat, 4.3g fiber

WW Honey Bananas
Makes 2 servings


Ingredients
2 bananas
2 tablespoons honey (or to taste)
granola cereal (optional)


How you make it:


1. Slice the bananas into two small bowls.
2. Drizzle honey over top; sprinkle with granola if desired.


Freestyle SmartPoints per serving: 1
Nutritional information per serving: 168 calories, 0.4g fat, 3.1g fiber

Makes 4 servings

Ingredients
1 (1/3 ounce) package sugar-free orange gelatin
1 (1 ounce) package sugar-free instant vanilla pudding mix
1 3/4 cups cold milk
1/4 cup boiling water
1/2 teaspoon vanilla extract

How you make it:

1. Combine the gelatin and the boiling water. Stir until dissolved.
2. Combine the cold milk and pudding mix.
3. Beat for 2 minutes with an electric mixer.
4. Add the gelatin mixture and vanilla extract. Mix well.
5. Pour into serving dishes or moulds. Chill until firm.
One serving is approximately 130 grams.

Freestyle Smartpoints per serving: 1
Nutritional information per serving: 97 calories, 4g fat, 0.1g fiber

Makes 20 small cakes

Ingredients
Removed Skin of 500g salmon fillets,
Three tbsp. fine corn flour
One egg white
One tbsp. finely chopped ginger

Three Shredded kaffir lime leaves
Three tbsp. chopped flat leaf parsley
One tsp wasabi
For the lime dipping sauce
1/4 cup lime juice
1/4 cup soy sauce
Two tbsp. brown sugar

How you make it:

- To make the salmon cakes, take off any bones from the salmon and cut into One-quarter inch dices.

- Mix the the egg white with chopped salmon, lime leaves, corn flour, ginger, chopped parsley and wasabi paste; mix well.

- Fry the cakes in oil (or grill) on each side, until they turn golden brown. Drain the cakes on table towels, &

keep warm in an oven that is low until the batter have been cooked.

- Mix the lime juice, brown sugar, soy sauce to make the lime dipping sauce.

- The warm salmon cakes can now be served with the dipping sauce.

Freestyle SmartPoints for one cake: 0
Nutritional information for one cake: 44 calories, 0.9g fat, 0.1g fiber

Makes 6 servings

## Ingredients
250 g ground chicken
1 egg white, lightly beaten
100 g mushrooms, chopped
1 onion, diced
1 stalk celery, chopped
1 large parsley, sprig
1/2 cup breadcrumbs
2 teaspoons soy sauce, salt reduced
3 whole wheat English muffins
1 tomato
3 lettuce leaves

## How you make it:
1. Process the mushrooms, celery, onion, parsley, egg white and soy sauce in a food processor until smooth.
2. Mix this with the ground chicken and enough bread crumbs to make a soft, but manageable texture.
3. Divide the mix into 6 and then shape into balls.
4. On a baking tray lined with paper, press the balls down and place in a preheated oven.
5. Serve on a muffin half with the lettuce leaf and 2 slices of tomato.

Freestyle SmartPOINTS per serving: 1
Nutritional information per serving: 172 calories, 2.6g fat, 3.5g fiber

Makes 12 kebabs

Ingredients
2 chicken breasts
4 pieces bread
1/2 cup breadcrumbs
2 dried garlic
2 big onions
2 green chilies
1/2 teaspoon black pepper
salt (as required)
refined oil (for frying)

How you make it:
1. Put chicken, onions, garlic, chillies, black pepper powder and salt in the blender and run until mixture is totally smooth (add very little water if at all necessary).
2. Transfer the mixture to the bowl.
3. Add bread crumbs and the bread pieces (crush them thoroughly with wet hands); mix them well using your hands.
4. Heat the oil in a pan (fill almost 5 1/2 inches for frying).
5. Take out small scoops of mixture, make small balls and flatten them a little before putting in the oil.
6. Fry on medium heat on both sides until well done.

Freestyle Smartpoint for one kebab: 1
Nutritional information for one kebab: 95 calories, 2.8g fat, 0.9g fiber

Makes 10 servings

Ingredients
Dice two medium bananas
two cups grapes

Dice two medium apples
2 cups sliced strawberries
chop 1/4 cup pecans

Drain 1 (20 ounce) can pineapple tidbits, reserve juice
pudding mix

1 (1 1/2 ounce) box sugar-free instant vanilla pudding mix or
vegetarian sugar-free instant vanilla
1/2 cup water

How you make it:

- In a Big mixing bowl, mix the apples, bananas, and lemon juice.

- Turn until evenly coated.

- Add strawberries, pineapple, pecans and grapes.

- Combine pineapple juice and water pudding mix, In a Mixing Bowl using a wire whisk until smooth.

- Include pudding mixture to the fruit.

- Gently mix until thoroughly coated.

- Put in a Refrigerator until ready to serve, YUMMY.

Freestyle Smartpoints per serving: 1
Nutritional information per serving: 128 calories, 2.4g fat, 3.8g fiber

Servings: 4

Ingredients
Two minced garlic cloves
One tbsp. chili powder

One tbsp. herbs de Provence
One tsp. cinnamon
half tbsp. balsamic vinegar with good quality

One tsp cumin
four tbsp. olive oil with good quality

One and half lbs fresh pumpkin, seeded and cut after peeled into half inch cubes

How you make it:

- Set the Oven to 450°F to Preheat.

- Butter the baking dish (or you can try spraying an oven proof baking dish with non-stick cooking spray if you prefer).

- Mix the garlic in a bowl, Herbes de Provence, cinnamon, chili powder, cumin, olive oil and Balsamic vinegar.

- Toss well to coat after Adding the pumpkin.

- In the baking dish, set the pumpkin.

- In the center of a pre-warmed oven, Place baking dish twenty-twenty five minutes; after ten minutes you can now coat the pumpkin with any other coating left in the bowl.

- Pierce with toothpicks and serve Once roasted,.

Freestyle Smartpoints per serving: 3
Nutritional information per serving: 175 calories, 14.1g fat, 1.9g fiber

Makes 4 servings

Ingredients

Salad oil
8 corn tortillas

How you make it:

- Cut into six equal wedges after you must have arrange about eight corn tortillas in a stack.

- Set the pan on medium-high to high heat after Pouring about half inch salad oil in a deep 2 or 3-quart pan.

- Add tortilla pieces when the oil is hot enough to make a piece of tortilla sizzle, using a handful each time, and turn to separate.

- Cook about 1 to 1-1/2 minutes (until crisp); drain on paper towels after lifting from oil with slotted spoon.

Freestyle Smartpoints per serving: 1
Nutritional information per serving: 104 calories, 1.4g fat, 3.0g fiber

Makes 24 servings

Ingredients
1/2 cup shortening
3/4 cup packed brown sugar
1 teaspoon vanilla extract
2 cups whole-wheat flour
1 cup all-purpose flour
1 teaspoon baking powder
1/2 teaspoon baking soda
1/4 teaspoon salt
1/4 cup milk

How you make it:
1. In a medium bowl, cream together the shortening and brown sugar.
2. Stir in the vanilla.
3. Combine the whole wheat flour, all-purpose flour, baking powder, baking soda and salt, stir into the creamed mixture alternately with the milk.
4. Cover and chill dough until firm.
5. Preheat oven to 350 degrees F.
6. Grease cookie sheets.
7. On a lightly floured surface, roll the dough out to 0.125 inch thickness.
8. Cut into rectangles or circles.

9. Place 1/2 inch apart onto the prepared cookie sheets.

10. Bake for 10-12 minutes in the preheated oven, or until crisp.

11. Edges will be golden brown.

12. Remove from baking sheet to cool on wire racks.

Freestyle Smartpoints per serving: 1

Nutritional information per serving: 119 calories, 4.6g fat, 1.4g fiber

SERVES 1

Ingredients:

1/2 cup fat-free egg substitute

1/8 teaspoon salt

1/8 teaspoon black pepper

1 tsp canola oil

2 tbsp. shredded low-fat Swiss cheese

¼ cup frozen chopped asparagus, thawed

¼ cup frozen peas, thawed

¼ cup chopped red bell pepper

2 tbsp. chopped fresh chives or scallions

How you make it

1. Whisk together egg substitute, salt, and black pepper in medium bowl.

2. Heat oil in medium nonstick skillet over medium heat. Add egg mixture and cook, stirring gently, until underside is set, about 1 minute.

3. Sprinkle Swiss, asparagus, peas, and bell pepper over half of omelette. Fold unfilled half of omelette over to enclose filling. Cook until cheese is melted, about 2 minutes.

4. Slide omelette onto plate and sprinkle with chives.

PER SERVING (1 omelette): 181 Cal

6 g Total Fat, 1 g Sat Fat

0 g Trans Fat, 5 mg Chol

615 mg Sodium, 13 g Total Carb

4 g Fiber, 20 g Protein

206 mg Calcium

Freestyle SmartPoint value: 2

Ingredients
1 large pear
2 tablespoons no-fat cream cheese

1 tablespoon whole half pecans (or walnuts)
2 teaspoons honey

Vegetable oil cooking spray
1/8 teaspoon salt

1/8 teaspoon nutmeg


How you make it:
1. Preheat the oven to 350 degrees F.
2. If you wish, peel the pear. Slice the pear in half lengthwise, and scoop out seeds to make a nice circle. Spray with cooking spray and set aside in a gratin dish sprayed with cooking spray, cut side up.
3. In a small bowl mix together 1 teaspoon honey, the cream cheese, nutmeg and salt. Fill each pear half cavity with half of the cheese mixture.
4. Place a half walnut or pecan on top of the cheese mixture, lightly pressing it down. Drizzle the pear halves with the remaining teaspoon of honey.
5. Roast the pear halves on the center grate of the oven for about 1 hour (or until soft). Test with a toothpick at about 45 minutes.

Servings: 2

Nutritional information for one serving:
Freestyle SmartPoints: 1
Calories: 156
Calories from fat: 68
Total fat: 7.6g
Cholesterol: 15mg
Sodium: 189mg
Total carbs: 22.8g
Dietary fiber: 3.5g
Protein: 2.1g

Ingredients
8 teaspoons jam or jelly or preserves (one-quarter tsp for each cracker)
16 teaspoons creamy peanut butter (half tsp for each cracker)
32 saltine crackers or Ritz crackers


How you Make it:
1. Smear the peanut butter, then the jam or jelly on the crackers.
2. Place the appetizers on a pretty tray and serve.


Servings: 32
Nutritional information for one serving:


Freestyle SmartPoints: 0
Calories: 32
Calories from fat: 15
Total fat: 1.7g
Cholesterol: 0mg
Total carbs: 3.8g
Fiber: 0.3g
Protein: 1g

Makes 12 servings

Ingredients
3 slices bacon, cooked, drained and crumbled
1 (15 ounce) can navy beans, drained
1/2 cup crumbled Blue cheese (2 ounces)
1 garlic clove, chopped
1/4 cup chopped onion
1 teaspoon chopped fresh thyme
1 tablespoon chopped fresh parsley
1/4 teaspoon salt
1/4 teaspoon fresh ground black pepper

How you make it:

1. Place the beans, garlic, onion, parsley, thyme, salt and
pepper in a food processor or blender and
blend until smooth.
2. In a bowl, combine the bean mixture with the bacon and
Blue cheese.
3. Serve with warm pita wedges or toasted baguette slices.

Freestyle Smartpoints per serving: 2
Nutritional information per serving: 97 calories, 4.4g fat, 3.8g
fiber

Freestyle Cucumber Sandwiches
Makes 32 sandwich triangles

Ingredients
1 large seedless cucumber
8 thin slices firm whole wheat bread, crusts removed
8 thin slices firm white bread, crusts removed
125 g unsalted butter, softened
1 teaspoon orange zest, grated
thin orange slices, to garnish
fresh mint sprigs, to garnish

How you make it
1. Peel the cucumber, cut in half lengthwise, and slice
crosswise as thinly as possible.
2. In a small bowl, combine the orange zest with the butter,
stirring until the ingredients are well
blended and the mixture is creamy.
3. Spread each slice of whole wheat bread with the butter
mixture, arrange a few slices of cucumber
on each slice and top with the white bread.
4. Cut each sandwich into 4 triangles.
5. Serving suggestion: Arrange the sandwiches on a platter
(alternating the brown and white sides of
the sandwiches) and garnish with orange slices and mint
sprigs.

Freestyle Smartpoint for one sandwich triangle: 2
Nutritional information for one sandwich triangle: 63 calories, 3.7g fat, 0.7g fiber

A very simple and delicious recipe that's perfect for breakfast or as an appetizer or snack! Only two ingredients, but such a tasty result!

WW Sausage Swirls
Makes 28 swirls

Ingredients
1 lb bulk sausage
2 (8 ounce) cans crescent roll dough

How you make it:

1. Open the cans of dough and place on a cookie sheet (trying to keep in one piece), unrolling carefully, and pinch all the edges together.
2. Cut the sausage roll in half, and spread it thinly over both pieces of dough.
3. Roll up the dough lengthwise and place it in the refrigerator for about 30 minutes (or until firm).
4. Preheat the oven to 375 degrees F.
5. Cut the rolls into 1/2 to 1 inch pieces and place the swirls 1/2 inch apart on the cookie sheets.
6. Bake for about 20 minutes (until golden brown and the sausage is thoroughly cooked).

Freestyle Smartpoints for one swirl: 2
Nutritional information for one swirl: 87 calories, 4g fat, 0.6g fiber

WW Roasted Garlic with Bruschetta and Cherry Tomatoes

servings: 6

Ingredients
One loaf Italian bread, sliced
One garlic clove
For the topping
Two cups cherry tomatoes, cut into quarters
One big tomato, diced

One roasted garlic clove, mashed
Three chopped basil leaves
One and half finely minced tbsp of carrots
One jalapeno, minced
1/4 cup red onion, minced
Half tbsp. caper, rinsed
One or Two tbsp. extra-virgin olive oil

How you make it
1. Toast the bread in the broiler or on the grill.
2. Rub with the raw garlic clove.
3. In a bowl, mix the topping ingredients together.
4. Serve the garlic rubbed bread with the topping on top.

Freestyle Smartpoints per serving: 0
Nutritional information per serving: 176 calories, 4.2g fat,
2.6g fiber

WW Ice Cream Sandwich

Makes 1 serving


Ingredients

1 whole honey graham cracker

1 tablespoon light whipped cream


How you make it:

1. Break the graham crackers in half.

2. On one half of the cracker, place a tablespoon of whipped cream and top with another cracker half; press lightly.

3. Place in the freezer until ready to be eaten.


Freestyle Smartpoints per serving: 1

Nutritional information per serving: 37 calories, 1.4g fat, 0.2g fiber

Makes 1 serving

Ingredients
2 eggs
1 tomato
4 basil leaves
salt and pepper

How you make it:

1. Adding two minced basil leaves, pepper, and a half tsp water, after beating the eggs slightly with fork.
2. Spray the pan with cooking spray, after heating and add the mixture.
3. Stirring and scraping the egg from the bottom of the pan, cook until the eggs get a creamy all through.
4. Plate and Slice the tomato top with the scrambled eggs, season with salt and pepper after garnishing with basil.

Freestyle smartpoints per serving: 2

One serving is approximately 233 grams.
Nutritional information per serving: 171 calories, 10.3g fat, 1.9g fiber

Makes 4 servings

Ingredients
1 1/2 lbs red potatoes (about 4 cups), quartered
2 cloves garlic, smashed
1 teaspoon dried rosemary
1 tablespoon butter
1/2 teaspoon kosher salt
1/4 teaspoon black pepper

How you make it:

1. Place the butter and garlic in an 8-inch square baking dish.
2. Microwave at medium-high (70%) for about 45 seconds (or until the butter melts).
3. Add the potatoes, rosemary, salt and black pepper, toss well.
4. Cover and microwave at high for about 15 minutes (or until the potatoes are tender).
One serving is approximately 175 grams.
Freestyle Smartpoints per serving: 1
Nutritional information per serving: 151 calories, 3.2g fat, 3.1g fiber

Zero Point Easy Deviled Eggs
Makes 12 deviled eggs


Ingredients
6 hard-boiled eggs, cooled and shells removed
1-1 1/2 tablespoon mustard
3-4 tablespoons mayonnaise
1 teaspoon horseradish
1 teaspoon sweet pickle relish
1 dash salt and pepper, to taste
1 dash paprika (optional, to garnish)
6 green olives, sliced (optional, to garnish)


How you Make it:


1. Hard boil the eggs; once they have cooled, slice them in half and place the yolks in a medium bowl.
2. Using a fork, smash the yolks until no lumps remain.
3. Add the mustard, mayonnaise, horseradish and sweet pickle relish.
4. Mix well, adjusting the ingredients to taste.
5. Add salt and pepper to taste.
6. Spoon the mixture into the eggs (or, for a fancier presentation, spoon the mixture into pastry bag and pipe into the eggs).

7. Garnish with paprika and/or olive slices. Serve immediately or chill for later.

Freestyle Smartpoints per serving: 0
Nutritional information per serving: 54 calories, 3.9g fat, 0.1g fiber

Yummy Oven-Baked French Fries
Makes 8 servings

Ingredients
16 ounces frozen crinkle-cut French-fried potatoes
2 tablespoons grated Parmesan cheese
1/2 teaspoon paprika
salt (to taste)
black pepper (to taste)

How you make it:
1. Preheat the oven to 450 degrees F.
2. Combine the parmesan cheese, paprika, salt and pepper to taste.
3. Place the potatoes in a medium bowl coated with cooking spray.
4. Sprinkle the potatoes with the cheese mixture, tossing well.
5. Arrange the potatoes in a single layer on a baking sheet coated with cooking spray.
6. Bake at 450 degrees F for about 13 minutes (or until tender).
Freestyle SmartPoints per serving: 1
Nutritional information per serving: 89 calories, 3g fat, 1.1g fiber

Makes 6 servings

Ingredients
2 ripe bananas
1 tablespoon lemon juice

How you make it:

- In thin slices, chop the bananas.

- Rub lemon juice around the banana slices.

- In the oven at 200 degrees F, to bake, put the banana slices on those parchment paper, turning every ½ hour and looking out for burnt slices.

- Take them off when they are crispy and let them cool a bit, after which you store them in an airtight container.

- Serve, Yummy!

Freestyle Smartpoints per serving: 0
Nutritional information per serving: 36 calories, 0.1g fat, 1g fiber

WW Apple Fritters
Makes 12 servings

Ingredients
Two apples (peeled, cored and sliced into rings)
1/2 cup milk
Two eggs
One cup flour
One tsp baking powder
1/4 tsp cinnamon
One quarts oil (for deep frying)

How you make it:

- Mix together the dry ingredients.

- Beat the eggs in a different bowl, then stir in the milk.

- Combine with the dry ingredients.

- In a Heavy bottomed deep pot or deep fryer, Heat the oil to 375 °F (190 °C).

- In a batter, dip the apple slices and fry, a few at a time, turning once, until they turn golden.

- Drain the apple rings on paper towels, and serve sprinkled with confectioners' sugar, and/or maple syrup.

- Freestyle Smartpoints per serving: 1

Nutritional information per serving: 68 calories, 1.3g fat, 0.9g fiber

Zero Point Cinnamon Munch

**Makes 12 servings**

Ingredients
4 cups Rice Chex or Corn Chex cereal
4 tablespoons butter or margarine
1/3 cup sugar
1 1/4 teaspoons cinnamon

How you make it:
1. Combine sugar and cinnamon; set aside.
2. Melt butter over low heat.
3. Add selected Chex cereal.
4. Heat until all pieces are coated.
5. Continue for 5 to 6 minutes.
6. Sprinkle half of mixture (cinnamon and sugar) over Chex cereal evenly.
7. Continue to sprinkle sugar mixture over Chex until all is covered.
8. Heat one minute longer.
9. Spread on paper towel to cool.
Freestyle Smartpoints per serving: 1
Nutritional information per serving: 93 calories, 3.9g fat, 0.3g fiber

Makes 8 servings

## Ingredients
8 crackers
50 g cheddar cheese
1 small brown onion

How you make it:
1. Slice the cheese and onion.
2. Place a slice of onion on each cracker and top with a slice of cheese.

Freestyle Smartpoints per serving: 1
Nutritional information per serving: 43 calories, 2.8g fat, 0.2g fiber

Makes 5 dozen

## Ingredients
1 lb confectioners' sugar
3 teaspoons butter or margarine, softened
2-3 teaspoons peppermint extract
1/2 teaspoon vanilla extract
1/4 cup evaporated milk
2 (12 ounce) cups semi-sweet chocolate chips
2 teaspoons shortening

## How you make it:
1. In a bowl, combine first four ingredients.
2. Add milk and mix well.
3. Roll into 1-inch balls and place on a waxed paper-lined cookie sheet.
4. Chill for 20 minutes.
5. Flatten with a glass to 1/4".
6. Chill for 30 minutes.
7. In a double boiler or microwave-safe bowl, melt chocolate chips and shortening.
8. Dip patties and place on waxed paper to harden.

Freestyle Smartpoints per patty: 1

Nutritional information per patty: 88 calories, 3.8g fat, 0.6g fiber

# WW Freestyle Weekly Menu Planner

| Day /Time | Breakfast | Lunch | Dinner | Desserts |
|-----------|-----------|-------|--------|----------|
| Monday    |           |       |        |          |
| Tuesday   |           |       |        |          |
| Wednesday |           |       |        |          |
| Thursday  |           |       |        |          |
| Friday    |           |       |        |          |
| Saturday  |           |       |        |          |
| Sunday    |           |       |        |          |

# WW Freestyle Glossary List

# Weight Watchers Freestyle Journal

This weight watchers Journal is easy to use and will help you immensely in achieving your weight loss Goals. Simply jot down the food that you eat and its point and then deduct it from your Daily Point balance. We have prepared a journal for you, where you can easily track your weekly Smart points allowance and Rollover Points.

Here is a sneak peak of how it looks

*Today's Goal* ........................ *Date* ........................

Age ................ Height ........................ Weight ................

| Food | Value | Balance |
|------|-------|---------|
|  |  |  |
|  |  |  |
|  |  |  |
|  |  |  |
|  |  |  |
|  |  |  |
|  |  |  |
|  |  |  |

Smart Point Total:

Rollover Point:

*Water* ○○○○○○○○○○  *Vitamins* ○○○○○○○○○○

*Protein* ○○○○○○○○○○  *Fruits/Veggies* ○○○○○○○○○○

*Exercise* ..............................................................

*Note* ..............................................................

..............................................................

..............................................................

Visit this links below to get one Now

My Weight Watchers Freestyle Journal 2018>> Amazon link>> https://www.amazon.com/dp/1948191172

My Weight Watchers Flex Journal 2018 >> Amazon Link>>

https://www.amazon.com/dp/1948191180

My Weight Watchers Freestyle & Flex Instant Pot Recipes>> Amazon Link>>
https://www.amazon.com/dp/1948191199

# Conclusion

- The best aspect of the weight watchers freestyle plan is there isn't any limit to the foods one can and cannot eat. So, when it comes to comparisons to other forms of weight loss diets, WW freestyle is easier to follow, as it also offers community support. It is an amazing plan for those people looking to lose weight without making drastic changes to their lifestyle.

- With up to four points daily roll overs, and more zero points food to save up on the allocated daily points, it is easier and more flexible than the older plans.

- The freestyle plan is great for vegetarians and sea food lovers with the added variety of fish (anchovies, arctic char, bluefish, branzino, butter fish, carp, catfish, cod, drum, eel, flounder, gefilte, grouper, haddock, halibut, herring, mackerel, perch, whitefish, pike, sardines, salmon, pompano, sea bass, smelt, tuna, tilefish, roe, sablefish, snapper, tilapia...)

- It would encourage creativity by encouraging one to make the most of the food available to them.

- The down side to this plan however is that while the previous plan was focused on weight loss, this new plan is concerned with healthy eating, and with a wider range of zero point food to complement, members could be basked in expending their whole points on others sources of foods with value points, and using the zero points foods as fillers.

- We have provided A weekly Menu Planner that you can print and use to jumpstart your weight loss goals.

  We wish you all the best, don't forget to drop us a review on amazon. Let's know what you think about this Diet Plan.

CPSIA information can be obtained
at www.ICGtesting.com
Printed in the USA
LVHW011810070119
603021LV00020B/1161/P